DATE DUE

OCT 29 09			

FOLLETT

HEAVEN AND MIRTH®

Adam
and the Apple Turnover

AND
OTHER BIBLE STORIES TO TICKLE YOUR SOUL

by Mike Thaler

Illustrated by Dennis Adler

*Equipping Kids
for Life*

Dedicated to
Scott and Esther Holmes,
for the spark.
With love,
Mike

ADAM AND THE APPLE TURNOVER
© 2000 by Mike Thaler for text and Dennis Adler for illustrations
FaithKids™ is a registered trademark of Cook Communications Ministries.

HEAVEN AND MIRTH® is a registered trademark of Mike Thaler.

Published in association with the literary agency of Alive Communications, Inc.,
1465 Kelly Johnson Blvd., Suite 320, Colorado Springs, CO 80920.

Cook Communications, Colorado Springs, Colorado 80918
Cook Communications, Paris, Ontario
Kingsway Communications, Eastbourne, England

Edited by Jeannie Harmon
Designed by Clyde Van Cleve

First printing, 2000
Printed in Singapore
04 03 02 01 00   5 4 3 2 1

Thaler, Mike, 1936–
        Adam and the apple turnover and other Bible stories to tickle your soul / by Mike Thaler;
                illustrated by Dennis Adler. p. cm. – (Heaven and mirth; 1)
        Summary: Five stories, written in a humorous vein, based on incidents taken from the Old Testament that
                focus on the importance of obeying God.
        ISBN 0-7814-3261-8
        1. Bible stories, English–O.T. Genesis. [1. Bible stories–O.T.] I. Adler, Dennis, ill. II. Title. III. Series:
        Thaler, Mike, 1936– Heaven and mirth; 1.
        BS551.2.T44   1999
        222'.1109505–dc21

                                                                                            99-34084
                                                                                               CIP

A Letter from the Author

Taking this opportunity, I would like to share with you how this book came about. Born sixty-two years ago, I have been a secular children's book author most of my life. I was also content to have a fast-food relationship with God from the drive-by window. At the age of sixty, I came into the banquet by inviting Jesus Christ into my heart. Since then my life has been a glorious feast. These stories are part of that celebration.

One night I sat and watched a sincere grandfather trying to read Bible stories to his squirming grandchildren. I asked him, "Aren't there any humorous retellings of Bible stories that make them vivid and alive for kids?" He rolled his eyes and said, "This is it." The kids rolled their eyes, too.

This made me sad, for the Bible is the most exciting, valuable, and alive book I know, as is its Author. So I went into my room, with this in mind, and wrote "Noah's Rainbow."

Since then God has anointed me with sixty stories that fire my imagination and light up my heart. They are stories, which I hope are filled with the joy, love, and Spirit of the Lord.

Mike Thaler
West Linn 1998

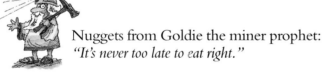

Nuggets from Goldie the miner prophet:
"It's never too late to eat right."

Author's Note

I have conscientiously tried to follow each story in word and spirit as found in the Bible. But in some cases, for the sake of storytelling, I have taken minor liberties and added small details, such as calling the fruit that Adam and Eve ate an apple. I pray for your understanding in these instances.

3

Genesis
Creation Celebration!

IN THE BEGINNING,
God decided to make a great poem
called the *Uni-verse*.

He made the heavens
and the earth.

Then He created light
and called it *day*.
He left a little dark,
and called it *night*.

On the second day,
He made wet and dry.
The dry He called *sky*.
The wet He called *water*.

On the third day, God who was neat,
put all the water into little piles
and called them *seas.*

Wherever there wasn't any water,
He called it *land.*

Then God whose hobby was gardening,
made trees, plants, shrubs, bushes, flowers,
grass and corsages.
He felt this was a good day's work.

On the fourth day,
God made the sun, the moon,
and all the stars.

It was getting dark,
and He still had His hands full of stars.
So He threw them up into the sky
and they sprinkled all over the night.

On the fifth day, God created fish
to fly through the sea,
and birds to swim
through the sky.
God loved numbers
so He told them
to multiply, and
they did, except for
the amoebas,
they divided.

The sixth day was a big day for God.
  He created all the bugs and the beasts.
    Then He formed a man from the dust
    (sort of a big mud pie, a clod out of sod),
    gave him mouth-to-nose resuscitation,
    and called him *Adam*.

  Then God lined up all the new creatures
  and told Adam to name them.

  "You're an *ant*... you're an *anteater*...
  you're an *antelope*... you're an *antipasto*...."

  When he had named the last animal *zebra*,
  the man grew sad.

**"It's not good for man
to live alone,"** said God.

  "All the animals have dates
  for the garden party,"
  moaned Adam.
    "The lion's taking the lioness.
  The bull's taking the cow.
  The rooster's taking the hen.

But I don't have a date, 'cause I ain't got no mate."

"Well," said God, taking out one of Adam's ribs,
"how about . . . a woman?"

"Great!" smiled Adam,
"I have a bride from my side."
And he named her *Eve.*

On the seventh day,
after a busy week at the office,
God rested.

THE END

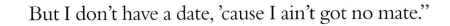

Nuggets from Goldie, the miner prophet:

"It's great to create."

For the real story, read Genesis 1–2:3.

Adam
and the Apple Turnover

GOD HAD TOLD ADAM AND EVE
that they could have their pick
of any fruit around them,
except the fruit from the tree
of the knowledge of good and evil.

"No problem," they agreed.

But when Eve was alone,
she went just to take a peek
at this forbidden tree.
And to her surprise,
a snake was in its branches.

"Aren't you the snake?" asked Eve.

"Yesss," hissed the snake. "Ssso, who are you?"

"I'm Eve," said Eve.

"Nice to meet you," said the snake, curling around the branch.

"Ever had an apple, Eve?"

"No," said Eve, "I've had plums, oranges, mangoes, but never an apple. God said not to eat the apples or we'll die."
"Sssilly," hissed the snake, "an apple a day keeps the doctor away."

"Maybe, but God said not to."

"How can you make apple pie, or apple ssstrudel?" hissed the snake, licking an apple.

"I'll give you all my recipes," he smiled.

"Well, maybe just one bite," said Eve. Munch. Munch. "These are good!"

"Ssshare them with Adam," smiled the snake, shaking the tree so that all the apples fell to the ground.

"What's for dessert?" asked Adam.

"Apple pandowdy," said Eve.

"Yum!" said Adam.

"Why didn't you dress for dinner?" asked Eve. Adam looked down and realized that he was naked. So he ran and put on a tie.

"Why are you wearing a tie?" asked God.

"I felt naked," said Adam.

"Have you been eating apples?" asked God.

12

"Just apple pandowdy," said Adam.
  "Eve made it for dessert."

"Is that true, Eve?"

"I got the recipe from the snake."

"Well, it's a recipe for disaster," roared God.
"That large worm is rotten to the core."

"Will we die?" stuttered Adam.

**"No, but from now on you and your children
are going to have to work for everything you get.
No more free rides. And as for that snake, he and
his children will wriggle on their bellies and eat dust."**
Then the Lord made garments of skin for them.

"You look good," said Eve.

"You're still the apple of my eye," said Adam.

"You better start planting," said God,
  "if you want to have breakfast."

THE END

Nuggets from Goldie, the miner prophet:
"When God asks you not to do something, you should listen."

For the real story, read Genesis 2:4–3.

14

Cain and Abel
Sibling Quibbling

Adam and Eve had two kids.
They raised a little Cain, and then had a little Abel.

Now Cain loved to grow things.
He would happily work in his garden all day.
He was very proud of his vegetables.

Meanwhile, Abel tended the flocks.
He loved his sheep
and enjoyed being a shepherd.

The two boys were
very happy doing their thing,
until one day they each brought
sacrifices to God at the county fair.

Cain brought his best cucumbers, and Abel brought lamb chops. Maybe God wasn't a vegetarian, because he liked Abel's offering much better.

When Cain saw Abel get the blue ribbon, he became very angry.

So angry that he took Abel into his garden and hit him with a zucchini until he died. Then he planted him.

When God saw Cain, He asked him, **"Hey, Cain, where's your brother?"**

"I don't know, I'm not able to keep up with him."

"I know you planted him between the sweet peas and the succotash," said God, **"so from now on your garden will be filled with weeds and moles. And furthermore, I'm kicking you out of the 4-H club!"**

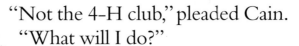

"Not the 4-H club," pleaded Cain.
"What will I do?"

**"You will just wander around,
and maybe become a lawyer,
an orthodontist, or a C.P.A.
Maybe you could raise
a little sugar, Cain,"** chuckled God,
who enjoyed His own jokes.

So Cain nodded, and headed east.
And since that time
there's always been trouble
between the homesteaders
and the cattlemen.

THE END

Nuggets from Goldie, the miner prophet:
"All good men are brothers, but not all brothers are good men."

For the real story, read Genesis 4:1–16.

Noah's Rainbow
The Zoo's Cruise

ONCE UPON A TIME ON THE EARTH, people became very naughty. They argued and fought and even killed each other.

This made God's heart very sad, for God truly loved His creation.

And as the naughtiness increased, God's sadness increased, until one day God grew so sad that He decided to destroy what He had made, and start all over again.

So God searched the earth and found one good man. His name was Noah.

God went to Noah and said, **"I'm going to send rain to the earth."**

"Should I get a raincoat?" asked Noah.

"Lots of rain," said God.

"Should I get an umbrella too?"

"A whole lotta rain," said God.

"Galoshes?"

"No," said God, **"you must build a boat."**

"Wow," said Noah, "that's a lotta rain. I'll make a rowboat."

"Bigger," said God.

"A sailboat?"

"An ark," said God.

"Wow," said Noah, "that's a big boat."

"Get started," said God.

So Noah quit his daytime job and started building a giant ark in his backyard.

"What are you doing?" asked his wife.

"You'll see," said Noah.

When the ark was finished, God told Noah to gather two of every animal, bird, and bug on the earth and put them in his ark.

20

"What about fish?" asked Noah.

"No fish," smiled God. **"The fish will be fine."**
So Noah gathered two of every animal, bird,
and bug on earth and brought them all home.

"What are you doing?" asked his wife,
"We already have a dog and a cat."

"You'll see," said Noah.

Then God told Noah to get on the ark
with his family and his pets.

"Where are we going?" asked his wife,
"We're miles from any
water recreation area."

"You'll see," said Noah. "You'll see."

Then God turned on all the faucets in heaven
and earth, and it began to pour. At first there were puddles.
Then the puddles became pools. Then the pools became ponds.
Then the ponds became lakes. Then the lakes became oceans
and lifted up the ark, and floated it over the mountains.

"By thunder," said his wife, "it's raining cats and dogs.
When will it stop?"

"God knows," said Noah.

21

The rain lasted for forty days and forty nights, and there was lots to do on the ark. All the animals had to be fed and the poop deck cleaned.

Luckily, Noah had his three sons—Shem, Ham, and Japheth— to help him, for he was a senior citizen. He had just had his 600th birthday party, and he was still tired from blowing out all those candles.

Then, as suddenly as it had started, the rain stopped, and the sun came out. The water of the earth receded till the peaks of mountains poked above the waves. Noah decided to send out a bird to see if there was a place to land.

The turkeys couldn't fly, so he decided to send out a dove. When the dove didn't return, he knew the land was dry. So he opened up the door of the ark and all the animals, birds, and bugs walked, flew, and wiggled down the gangplank.

And God said, "Noah, you are now
caretaker of all these creatures
and this brand-new earth.
And I promise
I will never do this again.
As a sign of my friendship and love,
I will paint an arc in the sky
with every color I know."

And Noah, his family,
and all the creatures looked up
and thanked God
as they saw
the very first
rainbow.

THE END

Nuggets from Goldie, the miner prophet:
"If you don't clean up your act, you could be all washed up."

For the real story, read Genesis 6–9:17.

Lot
Please Pass the Salt

LIKE CITY MOUSE AND COUNTRY MOUSE,
Lot was a city boy and Abraham was a country boy.
The problem was that the city
Lot picked to live in was full of sin.
It was the city of Sodom,
and when God came
with two angels to destroy it,
He stopped at Abraham's house.

"Where are you going, God?"
asked Abraham.

"To the city of Sodom," said God.

"I heard it's not a bad place to visit,
but you wouldn't want to live there," said Abraham.

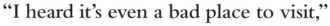

"I heard it's even a bad place to visit," said God. "In fact, it's so bad I'm going to destroy it."

"All of it?" asked Abraham.

"All of it," said God.

"What if You find fifty fine folks there?" asked Abraham.

"Well," said God, "then maybe I wouldn't destroy it."

"Good," said Abraham, "but what if you only find forty?"

"I'd spare it for forty," said God, shaking his head.

"How about thirty?" said Abraham.

"Are you bargaining with me?" asked God.

"No," said Abraham, "but surely if You find thirty righteous people, You wouldn't destroy them."

"You have a point," said God.

"In fact, I bet you'd spare the city for twenty good people."

"You're really pushing it," said God.

26

"You know, God, it's worth saving for ten."

"All right, all right," sighed God,
**"if I find ten good people in the city,
I won't destroy it."**

"What about ten in the city *and* the suburbs?"

"Good-bye, Abraham," said God,
"I'll see you later."

"Oh listen, God, be sure to say hello
to my cousin Lot."

So the angels of God
searched the city
and the suburbs of Sodom,
and they couldn't find
one good person.

They found
a couple of nice dogs,
and a sweet parakeet,
but pets weren't included
in the deal.
So they decided
to destroy
the whole city.

On their way out,
they stopped
to say hello to Lot.

"Stay the night," said Lot.

"We really can't,"
said the angels.
"We have a *lot* to do."

"A lot to do," laughed Lot,
"that's a good one. Listen,
just stay half the night."

"I guess pushiness is a family trait,"
chuckled the angels.

"Listen, just stay for dinner."

"All right, all right," said the angels, "we'll stay for dinner."

"And dessert, too," said Lot.

In the middle of dinner there was a pounding on Lot's door.
He opened it and found himself facing a drunken mob.

"Send out your guests," they shouted, "we're havin' a party!"

"Sorry guys, they only have time for dinner, dessert,
and coffee."

"Don't be party poopers!" they shouted
and they started to push by Lot.

The angels pulled Lot in
and slammed the door.
Then they opened the door
and struck all the drunken men blind.

"Hey, now we're blind drunk,"
said the men as they staggered away.

"Look," said the angels,
"gather up your family
and leave this town."

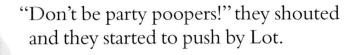

"You haven't had
your espresso yet."

"Now!"
thundered the angels.

"I haven't washed the dishes,"
said Mrs. Lot.

The angels grabbed Lot,
his wife, and their two daughters
and bustled them out of the city.

"Go!" they thundered.
"Don't stop till you reach those mountains,

29

and whatever you do,
don't look back."

"The mountains are very far,"
said Lot. "What if we only go
as far as that nearby town?"

"Okay, okay," said the angels,
"but get going. You're holding up
the whole show."

So Lot and his family quickly departed,
and when they reached
the nearby town,
the sky behind them lit up
as God rained fire down on Sodom.

"Wow!" said Mrs. Lot
turning around,
"I hate to miss the show."
Instantly she turned into a pillar of salt.

"She was always a salty old girl,"
said Lot, "and a pillar
in the community."

"Now that the city's destroyed,
maybe we can open a parking lot
and call it LOT'S LOT,"
said one of his daughters.

"Or," chuckled the other,
"we could call it CAMEL-LOT!"

THE END

Nuggets from Goldie, the miner prophet:
"When you don't obey God, there can be stiff penalties."

For the real story, read Genesis 18:16–19:29.

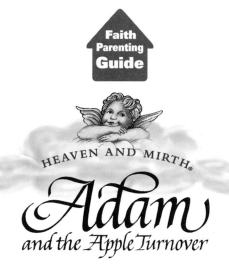

Faith Parenting Guide

HEAVEN AND MIRTH

Adam
and the Apple Turnover

Age: 6 and up

Life Issue: The importance of obeying God.

Spiritual Building Block: Obedience

Learning Styles

Help your child learn about obeying God in the following ways:

Sight: While driving, point out the different signs along the road to your child. Why are the road signs placed there? Why is it important to obey the signs? Talk about the confusion that would arise if everyone made their own driving rules.

Sound: Read the story of Adam and Eve from another Bible storybook. Have your child choose a character to role play and as you read the story aloud, let the child act it out. Talk to your child about the decisions his or her character made. Did they do what God told them to do?

Touch: Have a fun family outing by setting a destination for a favorite ice cream shop. Write the directions on index cards and give them to your child to read aloud. As each direction is given, do everything possible not to obey (turn left when directed to turn right, turn a corner when directed to go straight, etc.). Then talk about the confusion that comes into our lives when we choose not to obey God. End your trip at the ice cream shop.

Adapted from *An Introduction to Family Nights* by Jim Weidmann and Kurt Bruner, published by ChariotVictor Publishing, page 59.